Rubáiyát
of
Omar
Khayyám

Rubáiyát of Omar Khayyám

Rendered into English Verse by
Edward Fitzgerald

———∘∘∘∘∘∘∘∘∘———

Illustrated by René Bull

Gramercy Books
New York • Avenel

Introduction
Copyright © 1992 by Outlet Book Company, Inc.
All rights reserved

This 1992 edition is published by Gramercy Books
distributed by Outlet Book Company, Inc.
a Random House Company,
40 Engelhard Avenue,
Avenel, New Jersey 07001

Random House
New York • Toronto • London • Sydney • Auckland

Designed by Melissa Ring

Printed and bound in Singapore

Library of Congress Cataloging-in-Publication Data
Omar Khayyám.
[Rubáiyát. English]
Rubáiyát of Omar Khayyám / translated by Edward Fitzgerald.
p. cm.
Translated from the Persian.
ISBN 0-517-07232-7
I. FitzGerald, Edward, 1809–1883. II. Title.
PK6513.A1 1992
891'.5511—dc20
91-28331
CIP

8 7 6 5 4 3

Introduction

The *Rubáiyát of Omar Khayyám* is one of the most widely read poetical works in the English language. The quatrains were written in the twelfth century by a brilliant Persian polymath. They were forgotten for seven centuries until, by chance, they were read by a sensitive and imaginative English poet, who freely translated the verses which led to their great popularity in the West.

Omar Khayyám's *rubáiyát*, or "quatrains," reveal the poet as thoughtful and profound, a man plagued by the eternal questions of the nature of the universe, the passage of time, and the relationship of men and women to God. But who was Omar Khayyám?

The details of the life of the Persian poet, mathematician, and astronomer are sketchy. He was born in the middle of the eleventh century at Naishápúr in Khorassán, where he received an extensive education in the sciences and philosophy. His name, Khayyám, which means "tentmaker," may have derived from his father's trade. It is possible that he himself worked as a tentmaker until one of his former schoolmates, having risen to a position of eminence, granted him a yearly stipend. Free to devote himself to the pursuit of knowledge, it was then that he went to Samarkand, where he completed, in Arabic, his important treatise on algebra.

He became so well-known that he was invited by Sultan Malik Shah to undertake the astronomical observations necessary for the reform of the calendar. Later, he was commissioned to design an observatory in collaboration with other famous astronomers.

Rubáiyát of Omar Khayyám

After the death of his patron in 1092, Omar Khayyám went on a pilgrimage to Mecca. He returned to his native Naishápúr, where he taught and frequently served the court by predicting future events, a talent for which he was acclaimed. Although he was a brilliant man who mastered many subjects, when he died in 1122 he left behind only a few brief tracts on metaphysics, the treatise on algebra and one on Euclid, and a collection of verses.

In 1856, Edward Fitzgerald, a poet and translator, began reading the *rubáiyát*, which had been found by his friend Edward Byles Cowell, an amateur linguist and Middle Eastern scholar, among uncatalogued materials in the Bodleian Library at Oxford. Fitzgerald found in the verses some consolation for his unfulfilled marriage and recent separation and began to "translate" them. From Omar Khayyám's spontaneous verses Fitzgerald created a continuous sequence, sometimes compressing several of the original poems into one of his own quatrains. He imbued Omar Khayyam's *rubáiyát* with a dramatic unity, beginning with dawn and the desire to seize the pleasure of the passing moment, moving through the day until, at nightfall, he laments the fading of youth and the approach of death.

Fitzgerald's translation of the *Rubáiyát of Omar Khayyám* was first published anonymously in 1859 by Bernard Quaritch, a London bookseller. It was reviewed by the *Literary Gazette* but aroused little interest. Quaritch, in ever more desperate attempts to cut his losses on the 250 copies he had printed, gradually reduced the price from the original one shilling until the books ended up in his "penny box" outside the shop. From there they might easily have become wastepaper had not Dante Gabriel Rossetti come across a copy. Passing it around in London's literary circles, Rossetti set the *Rubáiyát* on the road to fame. In England, however, for at least twenty-five years the *Rubáiyát of Omar*

Rubáiyát of Omar Khayyám

Khayyám was little known outside literary circles. In the United States, largely due to the advocacy of Thomas Perry, a well-known editor and critic, it became widely known and read much sooner.

It was only after Fitzgerald's death in 1883, at the age of seventy-five, and the acknowledgement of the brilliance of his work by Alfred Lord Tennyson, that the *Rubáiyát* and Fitzgerald began to be greatly admired.

There have since been other, more literal, translations of the *Rubáiyát*, but there has never been one that is more beautiful. Coming to it not as a scholarly translator, but as a poet filled with the vitality of Omar Khayyám, Edward Fitzgerald succeeded in recreating his spirit—the fusion of delight and sadness.

The magnificent illustrations in this edition of the *Rubáiyát of Omar Khayyám* were done by René Bull. Born in Dublin in 1870, Bull was twenty-six when he became special artist for the English periodical *Black and White*, for which he covered the Armenian massacres and both the Greco-Turkish and Boer Wars. He also made trips for the paper to India and covered the Atbara and Omdurman campaigns, augmenting his on-the-spot sketches with written descriptions and photographs. He later used his first-hand knowledge of Easter costume and customs to achieve striking effects in his superb illustrations for the *Rubáiyát*.

GAIL HARVEY

New York
1992

I

Awake! for Morning in the Bowl of Night
Has flung the Stone that puts the Stars to Flight:
    And Lo! the Hunter of the East has caught
The Sultán's Turret in a Noose of Light.

II

Dreaming when Dawn's Left Hand was in the Sky
I heard a Voice within the Tavern cry,
*   "Awake, my Little ones, and fill the Cup*
Before Life's Liquor in its Cup be dry."

III

And, as the Cock crew, those who stood before
The Tavern shouted—"Open then the Door!
You know how little while we have to stay,
And, once departed, may return no more."

IV

Now the New Year reviving old Desires,
The thoughtful Soul to Solitude retires,
    Where the White Hand of Moses on the Bough
Puts out, and Jesus from the Ground suspires.

V

Irám indeed is gone with all its Rose,
And Jamshýd's Sev'n-ring'd Cup where no one knows;
 But still the Vine her ancient Ruby yields,
And still a Garden by the Water blows.

VI

And David's Lips are lock't; but in divine
High piping Pehleví, with "Wine! Wine! Wine!
Red Wine!"—the Nightingale cries to the Rose
That yellow Cheek of hers to incarnadine.

VII

Come, fill the Cup, and in the Fire of Spring
The Winter Garment of Repentance fling:
The Bird of Time has but a little way
To fly—and Lo! the Bird is on the Wing.

VIII

And look—a thousand Blossoms with the Day
Woke—and a thousand scatter'd into Clay:
    And this first Summer Month that brings the Rose
Shall take Jamshýd and Kaikobád away.

IX

But come with old Khayyám, and leave the Lot
Of Kaikobád and Kaikhosrú forgot:
   Let Rustum lay about him as he will,
Or Hátim Tai cry Supper—heed them not.

X

With me along some Strip of Herbage strown
That just divides the desert from the sown,
  Where name of Slave and Sultán scarce is known,
And pity Sultán Máhmúd on his Throne.

XI

Here with a Loaf of Bread beneath the Bough,
A Flask of Wine, a Book of Verse—and Thou
Beside me singing in the Wilderness—
And Wilderness is Paradise enow.

XII

"How sweet is mortal Sovranty!"—think some:
Others—"How blest the Paradise to come!"
*   Ah, take the Cash in hand and waive the Rest;*
Oh, the brave Music of a distant Drum!

XIII

Look to the Rose that blows about us—"Lo,
Laughing," she says, "into the World I blow:
   At once the silken Tassel of my Purse
Tear, and its Treasure on the Garden throw."

XIV

The Worldly Hope men set their Hearts upon
Turns Ashes—or it prospers; and anon,
　　Like Snow upon the Desert's dusty Face
Lighting a little Hour or two—is gone.

XV

And those who husbanded the Golden Grain,
And those who flung it to the Winds like Rain,
　　Alike to no such aureate Earth are turn'd
As, buried once, Men want dug up again.

XVI

Think, in this batter'd Caravanserai
Whose Doorways are alternate Night and Day,
How Sultán after Sultán with his Pomp
Abode his Hour or two, and went his way.

XVII

They say the Lion and the Lizard keep
The Courts where Jamshýd gloried and drank deep,
*   And Bahrám, that great Hunter—the Wild Ass*
Stamps o'er his Head, and he lies fast asleep.

XVIII

I sometimes think that never blows so red
The Rose as where some buried Cæsar bled;
That every Hyacinth the Garden wears
Dropt in its Lap from some once lovely Head.

XIX

And this delightful Herb whose tender Green
Fledges the River's Lip on which we lean—
* Ah, lean upon it lightly! for who knows*
From what once lovely Lip it springs unseen!

XX

Ah, my Belovéd, fill the Cup that clears
To-day of past Regrets and future Fears—
　　To-morrow?—Why, To-morrow I may be
Myself with Yesterday's Sev'n Thousand Years.

XXI

Lo! some we loved, the loveliest and the best
That Time and Fate of all their Vintage prest,
    Have drunk their Cup a Round or two before,
And one by one crept silently to Rest.

XXII

And we, that now make merry in the Room
They left, and Summer dresses in new Bloom,
    Ourselves must we beneath the Couch of Earth
Descend, ourselves to make a Couch—for whom?

XXIII

Ah, make the most of what we yet may spend,
Before we too into the Dust descend;
*   Dust into Dust, and under Dust, to lie,*
Sans Wine, sans Song, sans Singer, and
*   —sans End!*

XXIV

Alike for those who for To-day prepare,
And those that after a To-morrow stare,
  A Muezzín from the Tower of Darkness cries
"Fools! your Reward is neither Here nor There!"

XXV

Why, all the Saints and Sages who discuss'd
Of the Two Worlds so learnedly, are thrust
  Like foolish Prophets forth; their Words to Scorn
Are scatter'd, and their Mouths are stopt with Dust.

XXVI

Oh, come with old Khayyám, and leave the Wise
To talk; one thing is certain, that Life flies;
  One thing is certain, and the Rest is Lies;
The Flower that once has blown for ever dies.

XXVII

Myself when young did eagerly frequent
Doctor and Saint, and heard great Argument
  About it and about: but evermore
Came out by the same Door as in I went.

XXVIII

With them the Seed of Wisdom did I sow,
And with my own hand labour'd it to grow:
*   And this was all the Harvest that I reap'd—*
"I came like Water, and like Wind I go."

XXIX

Into this Universe, and Why not knowing,
Nor Whence, like Water willy-nilly flowing;
*   And out of it, as Wind along the Waste,*
I know not Whither, willy-nilly blowing.

XXX

What, without asking, hither hurried Whence?
And, without asking, Whither hurried hence!
  Another and another Cup to drown
The Memory of this Impertinence!

XXXI

Up from Earth's Centre through the Seventh Gate
I rose, and on the Throne of Saturn sate,
    And many Knots unravel'd by the Road;
But not the Knot of Human Death and Fate.

XXXII

There was a Door to which I found no Key:
There was a Veil past which I could not see:
    Some little Talk awhile of Me and Thee
There seem'd—and then no more of Thee and Me.

XXXIII

Then to the rolling Heav'n itself I cried,
Asking, "What Lamp had Destiny to guide
    Her little Children stumbling in the Dark?"
And—"A blind Understanding!" Heav'n replied.

XXXIV

Then to this earthen Bowl did I adjourn
My Lip the secret Well of Life to learn:
     And Lip to Lip it murmur'd—"While you live
Drink!—for once dead you never shall return."

XXXV

I think the Vessel, that with fugitive
Articulation answer'd, once did live,
    And merry-make; and the cold Lip I kiss'd
How many Kisses might it take—and give!

XXXVI

For in the Market-place, one Dusk of Day,
I watch'd the Potter thumping his wet Clay:
*   And with its all obliterated Tongue*
It murmur'd—"Gently, Brother, gently, pray!"

XXXVII

Ah, fill the Cup:—what boots it to repeat
How Time is slipping underneath our Feet:
    Unborn To-morrow, and dead Yesterday
Why fret about them if To-day be sweet!

XXXVIII

One Moment in Annihilation's Waste,
One Moment, of the Well of Life to taste—
    The Stars are setting and the Caravan
Starts for the Dawn of Nothing—Oh, make haste!

XXXIX

How long, how long, in definite Pursuit
Of This and That endeavour and dispute?
    Better be merry with the fruitful Grape
Than sadder after none, or bitter, Fruit.

XL

You know, my Friends, how long since in my House
For a new Marriage I did make Carouse:
*   Divorced old barren Reason from my Bed,*
And took the Daughter of the Vine to Spouse.

XLI

For "Is" and "Is-not" though with Rule and Line
And "Up-and-down" without, I could define,
*   I yet in all I only cared to know,*
Was never deep in anything but—Wine.

XLII

And lately, by the Tavern Door agape,
Came stealing through the Dusk an Angel Shape
*   Bearing a Vessel on his Shoulder; and*
He bid me taste of it; and 'twas—the Grape!

XLIII

The Grape that can with Logic absolute
The Two-and-Seventy jarring Sects confute:
  The subtle Alchemist that in a Trice
Life's leaden Metal into Gold transmute.

XLIV

The mighty Mahmúd, the victorious Lord,
That all the misbelieving and black Horde
  Of Fears and Sorrows that infest the Soul
Scatters and slays with his enchanted Sword.

XLV

But leave the Wise to wrangle, and with me
The Quarrel of the Universe let be:
   And, in some corner of the Hubbub coucht,
Make Game of that which makes as much of Thee.

XLVI

For in and out, above, about, below,
'Tis nothing but a Magic Shadow-show
  Play'd in a Box whose Candle is the Sun,
Round which we Phantom Figures come and go.

XLVII

And if the Wine you drink, the Lip you press,
End in the Nothing all Things end in—Yes—
    Then fancy while Thou art, Thou art but what
Thou shalt be—Nothing—Thou shalt not be less.

XLVIII

While the Rose blows along the River Brink,
With old Khayyám the Ruby Vintage drink:
*   And when the Angel with his darker Draught*
Draws up to Thee—take that, and do not shrink.

XLIX

'Tis all a Chequer-board of Nights and Days
Where Destiny with Men for Pieces plays:
    Hither and thither moves, and mates, and slays,
And one by one back in the Closet lays.

L

The Ball no Question makes of Ayes and Noes,
But Right or Left as strikes the Player goes;
And He that toss'd Thee down into the Field,
HE knows about it all—HE knows—HE knows!

LI

The Moving Finger writes; and, having writ,
Moves on: nor all thy Piety nor Wit
*   Shall lure it back to cancel half a Line,*
Nor all thy Tears wash out a Word of it.

LII

And that inverted Bowl we call The Sky,
Whereunder crawling coop't we live and die,
*   Lift not thy hands to It for help—for It*
Rolls impotently on as Thou or I.

LIII

With Earth's first Clay They did the Last Man's knead,
And then of the Last Harvest sow'd the Seed:
  Yea, the first Morning of Creation wrote
What the Last Dawn of Reckoning shall read.

LIV

I tell Thee this—When, starting from the Goal,
Over the shoulders of the flaming Foal
*   Of Heav'n and Parwín and Mushtara they flung,*
In my predestined Plot of Dust and Soul.

LV

The Vine had struck a Fibre; which about
If clings my Being—let the Súfi flout;
*   Of my Base Metal may be filed a Key,*
That shall unlock the Door he howls without.

LVI

And this I know: whether the one True Light,

Kindle to Love, or Wrath consume me quite,

 One glimpse of It within the Tavern caught

Better than in the Temple lost outright.

LVII

*Oh, Thou, who didst with Pitfall and with Gin
Beset the Road I was to wander in,
    Thou wilt not with Predestination round
Enmesh me, and impute my Fall to Sin?*

LVIII

*Oh, Thou, who Man of baser Earth didst make,
And who with Eden didst devise the Snake;
    For all the Sin wherewith the Face of Man
Is blacken'd, Man's Forgiveness give—and take!*

Kúza-Náma

LIX

Listen again. One evening at the Close
Of Ramazán, ere the better Moon arose,
  In that old Potter's Shop I stood alone
With the clay Population round in Rows.

LX

And, strange to tell, among the Earthen Lot
Some could articulate, while others not:
  And suddenly one more impatient cried—
"Who is the Potter, pray, and who the Pot?"

LXI

Then said another—"Surely not in vain
My Substance from the common Earth was ta'en,
   That He who subtly wrought me into Shape
Should stamp me back to common Earth again."

LXII

Another said—"Why, ne'er a peevish Boy,
Would break the Bowl from which he drank in Joy;
*   Shall He that made the Vessel in pure Love*
And Fancy, in an after Rage destroy!"

LXIII

None answer'd this; but after Silence spake
A Vessel of a more ungainly Make:
    "They sneer at me for leaning all awry;
What! did the Hand then of the Potter shake?"

LXIV

Said one—"Folks of a surly Tapster tell,
And daub his Visage with the Smoke of Hell;
    They talk of some strict Testing of us—Pish!
He's a Good Fellow, and 'twill all be well."

LXV

Then said another with a long-drawn Sigh,
"My Clay with long oblivion is gone dry:
But, fill me with the old familiar Juice,
Methinks I might recover by-and-by!"

LXVI

So while the Vessels one by one were speaking,
One spied the little Crescent all were seeking:
*   And then they jogg'd each other, "Brother, Brother!*
Hark to the Porter's Shoulder-knot a creaking!"

LXVII

Ah, with the Grape my fading Life provide,
And wash my Body whence the Life has died,
*   And in a Windingsheet of Vine-leaf wrapt,*
So bury me by some sweet Garden-side.

LXVIII

That ev'n my buried Ashes such a Snare
Of Perfume shall fling up into the Air,
*   As not a True Believer passing by*
But shall be overtaken unaware.

LXIX

Indeed the Idols I have loved so long
Have done my Credit in Men's Eye much wrong:
Have drown'd my Honour in a shallow Cup,
And sold my Reputation for a Song.

LXX

Indeed, indeed, Repentance oft before
I swore—but was I sober when I swore?
    And then and then came Spring, and Rose-in-hand
My thread-bare Penitence apieces tore.

LXXI

And much as Wine has play'd the Infidel,
And robb'd me of my Robe of Honour—well,
*   I often wonder what the Vintners buy*
One half so precious as the Goods they sell.

LXXII

Alas, that Spring should vanish with the Rose!
That Youth's sweet-scented Manuscript should close!
The Nightingale that in the Branches sang,
Ah, whence, and whither flown again, who knows!

LXXIII

Ah, Love! could thou and I with Fate conspire
To grasp this sorry Scheme of Things entire,
Would not we shatter it to bits—and then
Re-mould it nearer to the Heart's Desire!

LXXIV

Ah, Moon of my Delight, who know'st no wane,
The Moon of Heav'n is rising once again:
  How oft hereafter rising shall she look
Through this same Garden after me—in vain!

LXXV

And when Thyself with shining Foot shall pass
Among the Guests Star-scatter'd on the Grass,
And in thy joyous Errand reach the Spot
Where I made one—turn down an empty Glass!

Tamám Shud